ICE HOCKEY

Ronald Litke

RIGBY
INTERACTIVE
LIBRARY

Library of Congress Cataloging-in-Publication Data
Litke, Ronald.
    Ice Hockey / Ronald Litke.
        p.   cm. — (Successful sports)
    Includes index.
    Summary: Surveys the attitudes, skills, equipment, and tactics
involved in playing hockey well.
        ISBN 1-57572-074-4
        1. Hockey—Juvenile literature.   [1. Hockey.]
I. Title. II. Series.
GV847.25.L528 1996
796.962—dc20

                                                                96-7515
                                                                CIP
                                                                AC

Acknowledgments
The publishers would like to thank the
following for permission to reproduce
photographs:

Allsport USA/Glenn Cratty: pp. 1, 22;
Allsport USA/Harry Scull: p. 25; AP/Wide
World Photos/Bob Galbraith: p. 5; Bruce
Bennett Studios/©Bruce Bennett: pp. 10,
18, 26; Bruce Bennett Studios/©Scott Levy:
p. 12; Dave Black: pp. 8, 16, 20; Duomo/
William R. Sallaz: p. 2; Duomo/Paul J.
Sutton: p. 27; Focus on Sports: p. 13; Focus
on Sports/Jerry Wachter: p. 19; Hockey Hall
of Fame Archives: p. 28; Hockey Hall of
Fame Archives/Doug MacLellan: front
cover; David Madison: pp. 11, 14; Mike
Smith: p. 23; Sports Photo Masters/©Don
Smith: pp. 9, 29; UPI Bettmann: p. 24;

Illustrator: Stephen Brayfield: p. 7.

Visit Rigby's
Education Station®
on the
World Wide Web at
http://www.rigby.com

Contents

The Fastest Team Sport

There is no sport quite like hockey. Nothing can compare to the feeling of skating at great speed with the **puck** on your **stick** and the determination to score. Another thrill is making a great pass to set up a teammate for a goal or helping your **goalie** to stop a shot. Hockey combines all the dramatic moments and techniques of team sports, but there is one major difference. The playing surface of hockey is ice. And that makes the game fast and smooth. The action moves back and forth in seconds, and the direction of the puck does the same. That's why hockey is so exciting to play and to watch.

The first organized hockey league was formed in the 1890s. It was known as the National Hockey Association of Canada Limited (NHA). The league was made up of four teams: the Montreal Canadiens, the Montreal Wanderers, the Ottawa Senators, and the Quebec Bulldogs. In 1917, the NHA stopped operating, and the National Hockey League (NHL) was formed with the same teams. A fifth team, the Toronto Arenas, was later added.

HOCKEY FACTS

The Bill Masterson Memorial Trophy is awarded by the Professional Hockey Writers Association to the National Hockey League player "who best exemplifies the qualities of perseverance, sportsmanship, and dedication to hockey." The trophy is named for Bill Masterson, a player for the former Minnesota North Stars who died in 1968.

Not much has changed in the sport of hockey. It always has been a game of sticks and skates, five on five with a goalie for each team, and the hard-rubber disk known as the puck. From its original five teams, the NHL has grown to 26 teams. Millions of fans watch this fast-paced game in stadiums and on television. Hockey has spread throughout Europe, in warm and cold climates. In North America alone, there are more than 750,000 *amateur*, or nonprofessional, players, from preschoolers to college students. Hockey is perhaps the most popular sport in the Olympic Games.

The popularity of hockey comes from the joy of skating, the thrill of competition, and the satisfaction of playing with a team. Also, because it is played on ice, the skill of hockey depends more on the ability to skate—which can be learned—rather than on strength or height, which cannot. Wayne Gretzky of the St. Louis Blues owes his success to practice. His father told him, "Wayne, keep practicing and one day you're gonna have so many trophies, we're not gonna have room for them all."

His father was right.

Gordie Howe and Wayne Gretzky, perhaps the two greatest professional hockey players of all time.

Goals of the Game

Although hockey equipment has improved over the years and may look different than it did in the past, the purposes of a stick, skates, and pads have not changed. How a player uses the equipment is what counts. Of course, sports requires ability, but it also requires thought and preparation, learning and practicing. Because the action of a hockey game is so fast, there is no time to make up shots or for a player to try to win alone. Hockey is more fun, and winning is more satisfying, when the team works together. That's how the pros do it.

Count on Coaches

As good as professionals are, they still listen to their coaches. The Montreal Canadiens, who have won more **Stanley Cup** championships than any other team, consider their coach the most important member of their team. The coach can see what each player does best. That means he or she can combine the talent of all the players to create an offense that can score and a defense that can help the goalie, plus pull together the players to create team spirit.

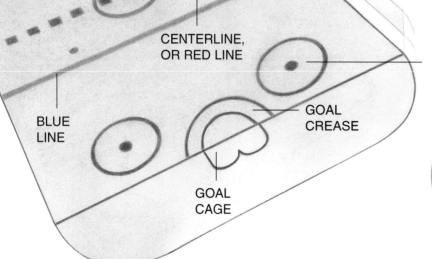

CENTERLINE, OR RED LINE

END ZONE FACE-OFF SPOT AND CIRCLE

GOAL CREASE

BLUE LINE

GOAL CAGE

Almost all professional hockey rinks are laid out like this one.

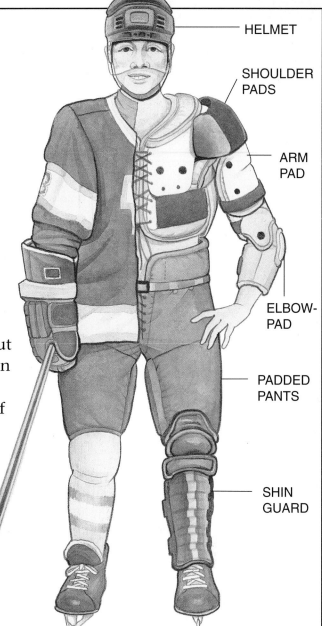

To play hockey, it is best to have full equipment. This includes a helmet and pads for areas at high-risk for injury, such as the knees and the midsection.

HELMET

SHOULDER PADS

ARM PAD

ELBOW-PAD

PADDED PANTS

SHIN GUARD

Get Ready to Play

If you're interested in playing hockey, it may be a long time before you actually join a team. You need time to learn how to skate, practice the basics, get in shape, and figure out what your skills are and what position you want to play. Each position in hockey gives equally to the success of the team. While many of the most popular players are the offensive centers and wings who score goals, the true heroes are playing defense. No matter how good the offense might be, if the other team scores more goals, your team will lose. As with most sports, it is defense that really wins games.

Great hockey teams have a balance of good offense and defense. Players from different positions help out all over the rink. And they adjust to each other as the conditions of the game change. A team must be as good **playing shorthanded** as it is on the **power play**, when it has an advantage.

Before you begin to play hockey, decide what your goals will be as a hockey player. These early decisions will go a long way toward your success.

Pointers

If you're thinking about playing hockey, talk about it with your friends, parents, and coaches. You need their advice and support to make the right decision.

Skating Skills

Skating is fundamental to hockey and is the most important skill to learn. If you can skate well, you can play any position and greatly extend the range of that position. Because players now skate better and faster than ever, they are expected to be able to roam the ice and help out where needed. Even goalies extend their range by passing and **clearing** the puck from the defending zone. However, they cannot do this if they do not skate well.

Skating requires balance, which is learned through constant practice of the basic techniques.

The basic skills of skating include the following:

The Forward Stride

Start with legs shoulder-width apart for balance. Bend the knees for comfort. Lean slightly forward and bring your body closer to the ice for stability. Push forward and downward, off the back leg, moving forward with the leg closest to the direction you want to go. Repeat, but with the other foot. Lift the legs just high enough so your skates clear the ice. This prepares you for the next stride. Practice often—without a stick or other equipment first—and your speed will increase quickly. Then try it with equipment.

The Stop

Off the forward stride, try to stop by quickly turning your body (and your skates) to a right angle and, with knees bent and feet still shoulder-width apart, pressing both skates hard into the ice. Try not to favor one leg, because both are needed to stop. Practice this on both sides.

Backward Skating

Stand with knees bent, shoulder-width apart, as if just about to lower yourself into a chair. Then slowly move your hips from side to side, bending slightly forward and pushing backward while leaning forward. This motion will force you backward. You can move farther to the left and right by pushing on the inside edge of the right skate (to go left) and the inside edge of the left skate (to go right). Your speed will increase as the motion becomes more smooth and you feel more confident.

Even after you feel comfortable with a skill, try it again, only faster. Always remember, practice makes perfect.

Pointers

The crossover is best practiced by tracing the number 8 into the ice. Each forward stride is followed by crossing one skate over the other to make the direction change. Doing this will help you become nimble enough to cross over to the left and right sides.

The *crossover* is the most important skill in skating. Mario Lemieux shows how it is done.

Planning to Practice

There are many levels of practice for becoming a complete hockey player. You should always try to make time to practice. Even if you cannot get to a rink, there are other ways to practice. Many hockey coaches demand that their players also learn ballet to better understand balance and movement.

If you can get to a rink, practice your skating skills. Also, work with the stick to learn how to move the puck and to pass it. It's best to practice with a coach; however, this is not always possible. Often you have to teach yourself and learn with friends or family.

Pointers

Your pre-game meal should be eaten no later than three to four hours before game time. This allows your body to digest the food properly for energy storage. Fruits, cereals, and grains—including pasta—washed down with two to three glasses of milk or water are great choices.

Crisp, accurate passing takes many hours of practicing correct timing.

Equipment Basics

Your equipment should fit properly. Your stick should have a **lie**—the angle between the blade and handle—that is comfortable for you. This allows you to handle the puck more effectively. The cuff of your gloves should cover your forearms for protection. Your shin pads must be strong but flexible. Your pants must have pads for your thighs and midsection, but they should not be bulky. Your shoulder pads should fit snugly but should have room for your arms to move. Above all, don't ever practice or play without a helmet and a mouthguard.

Practicing Techniques

When you practice by yourself, spend equal time doing skating drills (with and without a stick and puck); stickhandling with the puck; trying various shots; and passing toward targets for different lengths and angles, from a standing position and while moving. This routine will allow you to build your skills in the right order for becoming a complete player.

When you practice with friends, switch positions from offense to defense and from giving to receiving passes. Also, it is a good idea to race. This helps to make the skating drills, such as crossovers, skating backward, and stopping in the shortest distance, even more challenging. If you have the proper equipment, take turns at being goalie. This helps you get over any fear of the puck, no matter how fast it comes at you.

Practicing hockey is like learning anything else. It only looks difficult if you are inexperienced.

It's helpful to learn all the positions. If you can get the equipment, take turns playing goalie with your friends. This kind of practice makes you a more well-rounded player and gives you a better understanding of the game.

Shots that Score

There are a lot of shots in hockey. And using them effectively involves much more than strength: accuracy is just as important as power. During an actual game, even the best players may not get more than four or five chances to shoot at the goal. So it is important to make the most of any opportunity.

The actual power behind shots is not in the arms as you might expect. Learning how to shift your weight from the back foot to the front foot at the right moment—using your entire body—is what gives any shot its power.

The key shots in hockey include the following:

The Forehand Wrist Shot

This is the most common shot in hockey and may be the most accurate. The wrist shot is a great shot from anywhere from 10 to 40 feet away from the goal. Begin this shot by positioning yourself and the stick at a right angle to the puck. Then, placing the puck at the heel of the stick, start a sweeping motion. Transfer your weight from your back leg to your front leg and turn over your wrists hard just as your weight shifts, keeping the puck on the stick until the last moment. Follow through completely, bringing your rear leg up for balance. Your follow-through will determine your accuracy. Practice this shot first while standing still, then while moving forward.

The wrist shot is the most versatile shot. With a quick thrust of the wrists forward, you can make the puck travel low, fast, and accurately. The wrist shot is a hard shot to stop.

Pointers

When practicing hockey, examine the type of play with which you feel most competitive. Many players who like the speed of hockey want to chase the puck wherever it goes. Others like to watch the play in front of them and choose their opportunities—whether to score or to break up an opponent's play.

The Slap Shot

Everyone wants to perfect this shot, but it takes practice. Position yourself and the stick at a right angle to the puck. Bring the stick backward to about waist level (keeping the blade turned down), then shift your weight from your back leg to your front leg. The point of impact (aim just behind the puck) comes just as you reach the middle of the swing. Then follow through. This shot also causes your rear leg to lift for balance.

The Backhand Shot

Though not as powerful as forehand shots, backhands are still very accurate. And they allow you to lift the puck over the goalie's pads or stick. There are several kinds of backhands that are actually just different forms of the forehand wrist shot. By simply reversing the motion of the forehand, you can sweep a backhand (the motion feels more like pulling), or simply snap your wrists for a quick flick at the goal.

The slap shot is best practiced by lining up a series of pucks and hitting each one to a different spot in the net. By changing the speed and depth of your windup, you can develop great accuracy.

Picking Your Position

Hockey may look like a free-flowing and unorganized game, because the action is so fast. Unlike football or baseball—but a lot like basketball—hockey demands that its players roam all over the playing surface but stay within their assigned responsibilities. When considering a position to play, think about what best suits your abilities and range.

Offensive players have several key responsibilities. These include setting up plays, **forechecking**, passing, scoring, and helping out on defense. These tasks require strong skating ability and endurance, because offensive players make the most sudden changes of direction.

Playing defense comes with an understanding for the tougher parts of the game, such as **digging** for the puck, blocking shots, and having a lot of body contact. Being a goalie is similar to being a catcher in baseball. The goalie is often the team leader, because that position requires someone who takes the greatest responsibility—stopping the other team from scoring. Every position has its rewards.

As hockey has evolved, several players have changed the way people think about certain positions and how to play the game. Jean Beliveau, the great **center** of the Montreal Canadiens (1951–1971), could start up the offense from inside his own defending zone by helping to pick away the puck from the other team's offense. In the 1985–1986 season, Edmonton Oilers' defenseman Paul Coffey, who later joined the Detroit Red Wings, set a record by scoring 48 goals as a defenseman. He is able to handle his defensive responsibilities and contribute offensively. Coffey is second in **assists** among active players, with 934, behind only Wayne Gretzky.

On the other hand, fans today appreciate good defense. One of professional hockey's greatest players, Ken Dryden, rewrote the record book for goalies in the 1970s. He led the Canadiens to six Stanley Cup championships in only eight years. He also earned the **Vezina Trophy**, the award for the best goaltender, five times. A great defensive player can turn an entire team around. When Pierre Pilote joined the Chicago Blackhawks in the 1955–1956 season, the team steadily improved in the standings and won the Stanley Cup only four seasons later.

HOCKEY FACTS

Professional hockey has two halls of fame. The Hockey Hall of Fame in Toronto, Canada, was established in 1943. It includes not only players but also referees, linesmen, owners, and reporters. The United States Hockey Hall of Fame in Eveleth, Minnesota, opened in 1973 and also includes players, coaches, and other people involved in the sport.

This is the opening formation of players: the center, the left wing, the right wing, the left and right defenders, and the goalie.

Playing by the Rules

Hockey is a contact sport, no doubt about it. But the best players are those who observe the rules and prefer to play instead of fight. You won't see top players such as Wayne Gretzky, Pavel Bure of the Vancouver Canucks, or Brett Hull of the St. Louis Blues among the leaders in **penalty minutes.**

Penalties in hockey are severe. A player who is penalized must leave the ice, forcing his or her team to be shorthanded for at least two minutes. During this time, the opposing team has a clear advantage to score.

The rules of hockey are not as complicated as they are in some other sports. Hockey is a lot like soccer being played at a very fast pace. A professional game lasts 60 minutes, or three 20-minute periods. Amateur league periods range from 10 to 15 minutes. Overtime play varies by the type of league. In the pros, if the game ends in a tie, the teams play a 5-minute "sudden death overtime." The first team to score wins. If neither team scores, the game ends in a tie.

Some of the most exciting plays come from the face-off. In this play, the center tries to draw the puck back to the right wing, who is positioned for a quick shot at the goal.

The main rules in hockey are **offside** rules. A team is ruled offside when a player passes the puck across two lines (red and blue). The other offside situation occurs when a player gets into the attacking zone before the puck does. When these plays are stopped, a **face-off** occurs either at the point of the penalty or outside the defending zone.

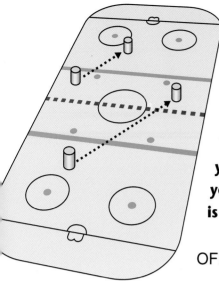

You will be called *offside* if you (a) pass the puck to a teammate across two lines or (b) go across the blue line and into the attacking zone before the puck does.

You will be called for *icing* if, while playing defense, you shoot the puck from your half of the ice past your opponents' red goal line, and an opponent who is not the goalie touches it.

OFFSIDE

Icing is an illegal defensive play. Any time a defending player shoots the puck across three lines (center, blue, and goal lines), "icing" is called. The puck is then brought back for a face-off in the offensive team's end zone. Icing is most frequently used to stop an offensive attack, but the puck just comes right back for the face-off.

ICING

Sometimes penalties happen by accident; however, they can be prevented by following some simple suggestions:

- Don't hold onto another player or his or her stick.

- Don't trip another player in any way.

- Don't use your stick to stop a player in any way.

- Don't throw your body at an opponent.

Penalties such as holding, tripping, **hooking**, spearing, elbowing, **cross-checking**, and fighting are generally used by players who are trying to make up for their lack of ability.

HOCKEY FACTS

The 1991–1992 NHL season saw many developments, including video replays to determine goals, the changing of the goal crease from a rectangle to a semicircle, and the disallowing of goals by any offensive player who stands on the goal crease line, is in the crease, or has a stick in the crease.

Getting in the Game

Today, there are hockey leagues for all ages. Local schools, park districts, and national amateur hockey associations, such as USA Hockey, may organize leagues in your area. Whatever type of league you join, it is important to join a team that shows a willingness to work for the benefit of the whole team.

Working with a Coach

Becoming a good hockey player involves listening to the coach almost as much as playing the game. A good coach is patient but firm with players. He or she offers criticism that does not hurt feelings but rather inspires players to perform better. A coach is a kind of a teacher, because in hockey you must learn the basic skills in a certain order if you want to become a complete player. The coach is your guide to learning those skills and to becoming a better player.

Pointers

Nutrition is important no matter who you are. But athletes especially need extra calories. However, that does not mean they should eat "junk food," which has large amounts of sugar, fat, or both. A balanced diet that includes whole grains, fruits, vegetables, and white meat, such as chicken or turkey, is the way to go.

The goalie is usually the center of attention in the game.

Understanding Teamwork

The idea of teamwork is also important to understand. No single player, no matter how good, can win a game alone. Successful teams find ways to combine individuals' strengths while limiting their weaknesses. The discipline of practicing with a team will teach you to rely on your teammates to help you, to give you a pass when you're open, or to come back and support the defense.

When the Montreal Canadiens won the Stanley Cup five seasons in a row (1955–1960)—a record that has yet to be matched—the individual players had not always been at the top of the statistics lists. But as a unit, they were virtually unstoppable. From their goalie, Jacques Plante, to hall-of-famers, such as Maurice "Rocket" Richard and Jean Beliveau, to amazingly consistent players such as Bernie "Boom Boom" Geoffrion and André Pronovost, the Canadiens became the model for the modern hockey team. They did not fight very much, but they played aggressively and were determined to win.

Every team, no matter what level, develops its own style. The satisfaction gained in playing hockey does not always come from winning, but from playing your best. Some days, your team will come out on top. On others, it will be a different story. That's what makes competition so interesting.

Bobby Orr, who played for the Boston Bruins and Chicago Blackhawks (1966–1979), was the first defenseman to carry the puck like an offensive player. He changed the way defensemen have played by expanding their range.

Opening the Offense

There may be only three assigned offensive players, but today's hockey demands that every player—even the goalie—gets in on the scoring. The basic strategy of using a center and two wings to score, with defensive players only to back them up, is no longer enough.

Nowadays, the offense begins from wherever the team gets possession of the puck. A team's ability to convert from defense to offense—"the transition game"—can quickly open up a game.

A power play is possible when one team has more players on the ice than the other.

To be able to take advantage of scoring opportunities, a team has to be prepared with plays and has to be able to execute those plays with the right timing. For all this to happen, each player must understand his or her position on offense. The **wings** usually trail up and down the ice on the right or left side. Meanwhile, the center roams the ice to get the puck and set up the wings. Sometimes, the wings approach the attacking zone straight ahead, and the center waits for them to cut toward the goal for a pass.

If they skate well, centers and wings can exchange positions by crossing in front of each other, confusing the defense with **drop** or **backhand passes** to set up clear shots. The more offensive players move *without the puck,* the better their chances of becoming open for a shot.

The basic positioning for the offense is a triangle among the center and wings. The defensive players position themselves at the top of the attacking zone. When the triangle of offensive players is spread properly, the other team's defense shouldn't be able to clog the passing lanes. Sometimes the offense is able to get in close or to push the puck back to a defensive player for a slap shot, maybe getting a rebound off a save and scoring.

An offense is only successful when the whole team plays together. That means moving the puck around to the open player. Or, if a player has the puck in good range, shooting it. Sometimes, offensive players may get checked or have to take some roughness from the defense while they're trying to score—but that's all part of the game.

In the power play, the offense takes advantage of the other team being shorthanded. Because there is more room in the attacking zone, players have the option to pass or move in, confusing the defense and moving closer toward the goal for a better shot.

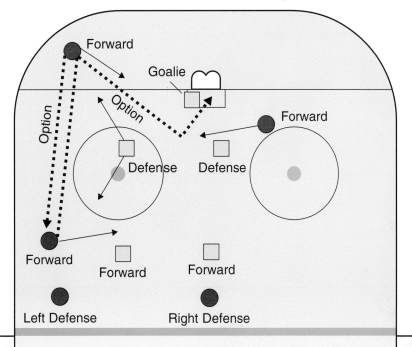

Durable Defense

The most basic rule of defense is this: the puck may get past you, and the other player may get past you, but never let both past you at the same time. Just as offense begins the moment a team gets possession of the puck, defense begins the moment a team loses the puck.

In defense, there are left and right positions as well as a goalie. But all six players on a team should be involved with defense. There are defensive plays, too. As in basketball, there can be **zone coverage**, where each player has a responsibility for a certain portion of the ice. Or there can be one-on-one coverage. But because situations in hockey change so fast, one-on-one isn't always a reliable strategy.

A complete defensive strategy covers the whole ice. The first line of defense is actually the offensive players. They must **forecheck**, which means they must go into the opponent's defending or center zone, chase down the player who has the puck, and try to poke it away with different moves of their sticks. In such a situation, a defensive player could turn right around and be on offense.

Chris Chelios of the Chicago Blackhawks is one of the finest all-around defense players in the NHL today. He combines a tough defense with the ability to assist and score goals.

But real defense takes place in the defending zone when the opponent is attacking. Defensive players are often the best skaters, because they change direction—backward and forward, left and right—more than the other players. Defensive players always try to position themselves between the offensive player and the goal.

Sometimes it may be necessary to **body-check** the opponent to prevent him or her from reaching the puck. In such cases, a player has to be sure to make contact. If contact is not made, the other player will get by. Checking is best accomplished by moving a shoulder or hip into the other player, staying low. After the check, the player gets back in the play by going for the puck or watching the goal.

The best defensive players are not afraid to try to block a shot with their sticks, skates, or pads. To block a shot, a player must move in close to lessen the angle of the shot and either poke with the stick or move in front of the puck. A player can take the puck on the pads or skates. Blocking a goal can often be more important than scoring.

Pointers

Practice backward skating with players coming at you from your right and left sides. By doing this, you will develop defensive skills for both sides of the rink.

Guarding the Goal

The goalie guards the smallest but most important space on the ice. Goaltending is one of the most difficult and challenging positions in sports. It requires concentration, quickness while wearing heavy equipment, an ability to catch like a baseball player, and coolness in the face of a speeding puck.

Goalies are the only players who do not get a break during a game. No matter how intense any single play is, the goalie always has to be ready for another shot.

Although they are the last line of defense, goalies do not work alone. The defensive players must understand their responsibilities to the goalie and how they cover the area around the goal. The goalie must never be left alone when the opponent has the puck in the defending zone. If one defensive player goes into the corner to dig for the puck, the other should take position in front of the net.

Pointers

A goalie's skates are the best defense against low shots to the corners of the net. But to be effective, the goalie must keep his or her skate blade on the ice, or the puck may slip underneath.

Terry Sawchuk, who played with five teams in his 21-year career, leads all goaltenders with 103 shutouts.

Communication between goalies and defensive players is essential. Goalies should constantly talk to defensive players. They can help them get to the right position or perhaps predict how an offensive play might be stopped before it becomes trouble.

When all is said and done, it's up to the goalie to stop the shot. To do this, goalies have to remain standing as much as possible. Once a goalie's body is on the ice, the net is wide open. To narrow the chances for an offensive shot, the goalie should "cut down the angle" of the shot. That is, the goalie should move toward the shooter to give him or her less room to shoot.

As much as possible, goalies should try to position their bodies centered on the puck, not the shooter. That allows for the most chances—with body, stick, and glove—to stop the shot.

Being a goalie takes hours of practice. Teams should line up a dozen pucks and have them shot quickly in succession with different types of shots and at different angles and points toward the goal. When a goalie can hold back this kind of attack, he or she is truly ready for the game.

Dominik Hasek of the Buffalo Sabres allowed only 1.95 goals per game in the 1993–1994 season. That was the first time in 20 years that any goalie had an average under 2 goals per game.

Olympic Glory

Some of the most exciting hockey games ever played have been during the Winter Olympics. Ice hockey was introduced to the Games in 1920 in Antwerp, Belgium, just after the first World War. The Canadian team defeated the United States, Sweden, and Czechoslovakia to win the gold medal.

The 1920 Olympics were the beginning of Canada's domination of the sport through 1952. After that, the former Soviet Union (U.S.S.R.) became a powerful team with a new style of strong skating, sharp passing, and quick shooting that changed the way hockey was played. Between 1956 and 1984, the Soviet Union played 52 games, winning 46 times with only 4 defeats and 2 ties.

The 1994 Olympic hockey gold medal was won by the Swedish hockey team. Its victory returned the style of international play to more passing and finesse.

The Soviet team's amazing run was broken only twice. The United States took the gold in 1960 and 1980, when the Games were in held in America. Both of these U.S. teams were quite scrappy. Fans worried they could not outplay the Soviets. But what the team lacked in talent, it made up for with hustle and determination.

Pointers

To master ice hockey, it isn't enough to just play and watch. While playing helps to learn the discipline of practice and the meaning of teamwork, and watching hockey games can show you the result of all the hard work the pros put in, reading can show you even more. Many professional players have written books that discuss their techniques.

The 1980 series in Lake Placid, New York, was perhaps the U.S. team's greatest. It was ranked seventh before the Games began, but it came from behind in nearly every game to win the early rounds. The U.S. coach, Herb Brooks, believed in discipline. The U.S. team entered the gold-medal round running on high emotion.

It was surprising enough that the U.S. team reached a 2–2 tie with Finland and earned a match with the U.S.S.R. The Soviets scored first, as expected, but the United States tied the game within five minutes. Only three minutes later, close to the end of the first period, the Soviets scored again. But the U.S. team again tied the score on a **tip-in**.

The 1980 U.S. hockey team won the gold medal in Lake Placid, New York, against long odds. Thus their nickname, the "Miracle on Ice."

The Soviets opened the second period with a power play goal and held a 3–2 lead into the final period. But at 8:39 of the third, U.S. winger Mark Johnson poked the puck loose from a Soviet defender and scored. And only 1½ minutes later, U.S. captain Mike Eruzione hit a slap shot past Soviet goalie Vladimir Myshkin for a 4–3 victory. The United States went on to win the gold by defeating Finland, 4–2, two days later.

Path to the Pros

While the teams of the National Hockey League only come from North America, the players come from many different countries. There are more Americans in the game than ever before, but there are also more players from Europe, including the Czech Republic, Slovakia, Finland, Germany, Norway, Ukraine, Kazakhstan, Belarus, and Estonia. There also have been a few players **drafted** from England, Korea, and Japan.

Still, most players drafted by the NHL come from Canada. They number more than 3 to 1 over Americans. They come from minor leagues, such as the Ontario Hockey League, the Western Hockey League from teams in American and Canadian cities, and the Quebec Major Junior Hockey League, which plays only in Canada.

In addition, 52 American colleges have sent players to the NHL. While most players come from the University of Minnesota, Michigan Tech, the University of Michigan, and the University of Wisconsin, players have also been drafted from Harvard University, Yale University, and Cornell University. Young players who have excellent potential have been drafted from high schools in New York, Massachusetts, and Minnesota.

Willie O'Ree was the first African-American player in the NHL, playing for the Boston Bruins for two seasons beginning in 1957.

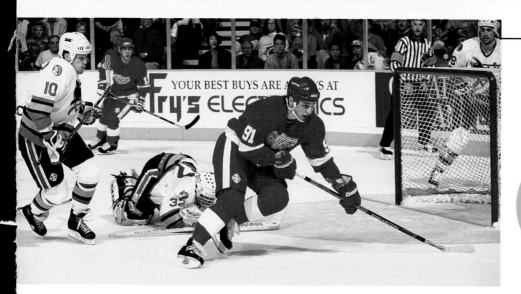

Most players come from colder climates, where the outdoor hockey season is longer. But there are professional teams in the southern and western regions of the United States (Florida, California, and Texas). And that usually helps to create amateur and school leagues that could lead a player to major colleges and maybe to the NHL.

Whether you're set on becoming a professional player or just out on the ice for some competition and exercise, hockey is a game you can work at your whole life. It's possible to improve your skating, shooting, and other skills over many years.

For Wayne Gretzky of the St. Louis Blues, his love of hockey started early and has not let up for 15 seasons. "I could skate at two. I was nationally known at six. I was signing autographs at ten . . . I turned pro and kept going to high school." But Gretzky's father also told him not to become "bigheaded." The greatest player in the game still says the highest compliment is that he "works hard every day."

Sergei Federov, a center for the Detroit Red Wings, was recruited from Russia. He is one of the NHL's top defensive forwards. His European style emphasizes the ability to play effectively on the entire rink.

HOCKEY FACTS

There are eight classifications of hockey play in the United States:
Mighty Mite: ages 6 and under
Mite: ages 7 to 9
Squirt: ages 10 to 11 (10 to 12 for girls)
Pee-wee: ages 12 to 13 (13 to 15 for girls)
Bantam: ages 14 to 15 (no bantam class for girls)
Midget: ages 16 to 17 (16 to 19 for girls)
Junior: ages 18 to 19 (no junior class for girls)
Professional: ages 19 and up

Glossary

assist The pass to the player who scores a goal.

backhand pass Passing to a teammate that is behind the player.

body-check Using the body legally to move an opposing player away from the puck by moving a shoulder or hip into that player.

center The offensive player in the middle who is responsible for setting up offensive plays.

clearing Generally a defensive technique in which the player moves the puck far away from any players.

cross-checking An illegal play in which a player uses a stick to check another player across the body above the waist.

crossover A skating maneuver in which one skate is placed over the other to change direction or increase speed.

digging Pushing out the puck from an opponent or along the side boards.

drafted The method by which a professional team chooses an amateur player, either from a college or high school, and makes an agreement that the player will play for that team.

drop pass A passing maneuver in which a player simply leaves the puck behind so a teammate can get it.

face-off Action by the referee in which the puck is dropped fairly between two players to start play or resume play after it has been stopped.

forechecking An action by the offensive players to get the puck away from the other team in their defending zone.

goalie The player responsible for guarding the net. The goalie has heavier padding than other players and uses a larger stick and a glove to stop and catch the puck.

hooking An illegal play in which a player uses a stick to grab another player around the arm or leg to slow or stop a play.

icing Shooting the puck over three lines to stop offensive pressure. Icing causes a face-off in the defending zone of the team that committed the error.

linemen The players who form a line. A trio of two wings and a center form the offensive line, while a pair of two defensemen form the defensive line.

offside When any player gets into the attacking zone before the puck does.

penalty minutes The amount of time a player spends off the ice because of a penalty

playing shorthanded When a team plays with four or fewer players because penalties have sent those players off the ice.

power play When one team has more players on the ice because of penalties, it has more "power" to score a goal.

puck The one-inch by three-inch piece of hard circular rubber that is the center of the game. A puck is frozen solid before game time so it won't bounce on the ice.

shift A period of time a player spends playing. A player can play several shifts in one game.

Stanley Cup The trophy that represents the championship of the National Hockey League.

stick Wood, fiberglass, or aluminum shaft, with a blade, that players use to move the puck.

tip-in Using the blade of a stick to deflect the puck and change its direction toward and into the goal.

Vezina Trophy The award given to the National Hockey League goalie who allows the fewest goals per game in a season.

wings Offensive players who play on the far left and right sides of the rink.

zone coverage A defensive setup of players that requires each player to cover a particular area and prevent offensive players from attacking.

Index